Empowerment Series for Young Women

by

LeEtta White

Published by
Vantage Point Publishing
3416 N. Shadeland Ave.
Indianapolis, IN 46226

ISBN 978-0-9849630-6-5

Printed in the United States of America

From the Author:

As a member of the Indianapolis Metropolitan Police Department for 30 years I have worked in a variety of positions, most recent being Community Relations Supervisor on the East District.

My heart has always gone out to the community even as a beat officer, my goal was to enhance the quality of life in the neighborhoods I patrolled and to help rid them of the criminal element that prevented growth in that particular area.

As a PAL (Police Athletic League) Officer I worked with many youth that had a sense of hopeless when we first met, and mothers who didn't know which way to turn, I put my heart into those youth and still have contact with some of them today.

As a Bike Officer on Downtown District I learned that circumstances beyond their control had placed some of our homeless women in the position they had found themselves in.

As a Detective Sergeant I came into contact with many women in bad relationships that didn't know how to get themselves out.

My experiences in Law Enforcement for 30 years have allowed the opportunity to recognize a need for guidance and direction to help build self-esteem, and provide resources for the women in our service district.

Most of our youth come from single family households, which is why my belief is that if we start working with the young mothers to assist them in turning their lives around then maybe the young men and women coming from these households will not turn out to be gang members, drug dealers, or addicts.

I've heard time and time again that you are a product of your environment; my vision is to change the environment in which these children are growing up in, to produce healthy and productive young men and women, and to give young women/mothers participating in the series a sense of pride and accomplishment.

Sergeant LeEtta White/Indianapolis Metropolitan Police Department

TABLE OF CONTENTS

Introduction:

Introduction

This women's empowerment series was designed with you in mind, there are so many struggles that young women face in today's society.

The empowerment series for young women will allow you to begin to take control of the things you allow in your life. We will discuss those sensitive issues like: Depression/Addiction, Domestic Violence, Breaking Bad Habits, Building trust and Bridging the gap with your local law enforcement agency, and finally moving in a new direction.

The empowerment series will allow you to set realistic goals for yourself, and also provide resources available to you, to help you meet those goals, whether it is: women to work programs, child care, parenting skills, GED or higher education, and the steps to take to receive the assistance you need.

Some researchers suggest that emotional intelligence can be learned and strengthened, while others claim it is an inborn characteristic.

This is a six week series that will give you the personal attention and support you need to address those sensitive issues and learn to strengthen your emotional

Chapter 1

Emotional Intelligence:

Emotional Intelligence… (EI) refers to the ability to perceive, control, and evaluate emotions. There are a number of testing instruments that have been developed to measure emotional intelligence, although the content and approach of each test varies.

There are four (4) branches of Emotional Intelligence…

Salovey and Mayer proposed a model that identified four different factors of emotional intelligence: the perception of emotion, the ability to reason using emotions, the ability to understand emotion and the ability to manage emotions.

1. **Perceiving Emotions**: the first step in understanding emotions is to accurately perceive them. In many cases, this might involve understanding nonverbal signals

such as body language and facial expressions.

2. **Reasoning with Emotions**: the next step involves using emotions to promote thinking and cognitive activity. Emotions help prioritize what we pay attention and react to; we respond emotionally to things that grab our attention.

3. **Understanding Emotions**: the emotions that we perceive can carry a wide variety of meanings. If someone is expressing angry emotions, the observer must interpret the cause of their anger and what it might mean. For example, if your boss is acting angry, it might mean that he/she is dissatisfied with your work; or it could be because he/she got a speeding ticket on the way to work that morning or he/she's been fighting with their spouse.

4. **Managing Emotions**: the ability to manage emotions effectively is a key part of emotional intelligence. Regulating emotions, responding appropriately and responding to the emotions of others are all important aspect of emotional management.

According to Salovey and Mayer, the four branches of their model are, "arranged from more basic psychological processes to higher, more psychologically integrated processes. (Kandra Cherry – psychology. about.com)

At the end of this chapter there will be a mix of self-report and situational questions related to emotional intelligence that will allow you to begin to recognize the challenges in your life that may cause a negative and/or positive reaction in your behavior.

I encourage you to use the spaces at the end of the chapters to make notes for your personal evaluation.

In my studies I learned that through some psychological research that it is very difficult for people to understand themselves without some kind of independent feedback.

So why measure emotional intelligence?

It can be used as an aid to self understanding and self –discovery. Sometimes learning who you are through self examination is a critical piece to making the necessary changes to a better life.

I realize that psychological and emotional stress can sometimes be overwhelming, and at that time it is essential that you seek outside help, but getting to know yourself and what things influence your behavior is a start to the ability to perceive, and control your own emotions.

Emotional awareness means knowing when feelings are present in yourselves and others; you have to be able to predict feelings in advance in order to control them.

Know what triggers a reaction in you, for example there was a time in my life that whenever I became angry I would tap my foot , and people around me that knew me would know that I was very, very, angry.

Or you might be one that taps your fingers when you are feeling impatient. Nature has provided us with a system eternally that guides our feelings, for instance we feel out of balance when negative feelings surface and things are not healthy for us.

If you fail to pay attention to your negative feelings or choose to simply ignore them they can cause you not to focus on the good feelings when they come, therefore, causing you not to focus on what needs to be solved.

No one likes negative emotions; therefore, so many people try to stop those emotions with drugs, alcohol, and even men. All these things defeat nature's purpose of supplying us with the eternal guidance system, and for nature's eternal guidance system to function you must acknowledge your feelings.

Once you can accurately identify your feelings, you can then identify your unmet emotional need and take the appropriate steps toward creating a healthier lifestyle

When you recognize and label your feelings you move it from the unknown to known, which makes it more manageable to deal with. It is much easier to deal with what you know verses what you don't know. And once you label that feeling you have now moved that feeling from the emotional section of your brain to the cognitive section.

And now that you know what the fight is, you know where to start the recovery. You have to fully accept your feelings as being real, and not suppress or deny that they exist, most times accepting your feelings helps prevent those feelings from coming back over and over again.

You must first predict your feelings so that you can make decisions that will lead to long term results.

I read that sensitive people living in abusive environments and insensitive cultures learn ways to numb themselves from their feelings because so many of their feelings are painful.

This statement is as true as any I've ever heard: I remember growing up in Clear Streams Garden an apartment complex on the south side of Indianapolis, which was called the "projects". I was in my early teens and I remember a woman whose spirits were so broken because of an alcoholic and abusive relationship she was in, I recall thinking "she's such a pretty lady, I don't know if she had people to talk to or to support her in her struggles but I do remember watching her and knowing I didn't want to be like her when I grew up.

Only to become that woman at the age of 24 with my first marriage, I had been a police officer on the Indianapolis Police Department two (2) years, had lots of friends on the department and lived on the district I worked in. I have now found myself in an abusive environment at home and what I thought was an insensitive culture on the job.

I first picked up the habit of smoking cigarettes for the first time in my life at the age of 27 to numb myself from the painful feelings I felt at home, being a police officer I felt I could not let my co-workers know that I was being physically and emotionally abused in my own home, so now who do I talk to, after all we deal with these types of issues every day.

My story is not an isolated incident every woman has a story you have the ability to write your own story and write your own ending.

Questions that help you identify your Emotional Intelligence:

1. I am aware of how each person feels about the other people in a social circle, in my group of friends?

2. I recognize my stressors'?

3. I am extremely anxious when involved in a confrontation?

4. I allow what others say about me and my abilities affect my outcome?

5. I feel uncomfortable around people I am not familiar with?

6. I become easily agitated with myself and others when I make a mistake?

7. When I can't think of what to say I become distressed?

8. I consider myself a good judge of character?

9. I recognize my skills, and talents?

10.   I am usually very quiet until I get to know a person?

NOTES

_____
_____
_____
_____
_____
_____
_____
_____
_____
_____
_____
_____
_____
_____
_____
_____

Chapter 2

Depression/Addiction

Thousands of women are diagnosed with depression every year. It is very important to recognize the symptoms and know that there is treatment available.

Most often women feel like they are alone in this struggle and that no one understands what they are going through.

There are clinical studies to prove otherwise. I have researched depression extensively and found that women are diagnosed with depression twice as often as men.

Depression in Women: contributing factors of depression in women can be physiological, social, genetic, or environmental, women also experience eating disorders, poverty, and sexual abuse at a much more alarming rate as men, which can also contribute to depression. One of the big pieces with women that lead to depression is...being the sole provider and caregiver.

From the University of Iowa health Care they wrote that seventeen percent of Americans will experience at least one depressive episode during their lifetime.

It's no longer a secret, you need to share your feelings with the people in your household and family, depression is real and it can be treated.

What is Depression?

Depression is a disorder that involves feelings of sadness lasting for two weeks or longer, often accompanied by a loss of interest in life, hopelessness, and decreased energy. These feelings can also affect your daily living activities and performance.

Depression is not "the blues" which is sometimes misleading to women; depression affects the mind where the blues is triggered by an unpleasant event or situation.

Depression is as real as diabetes and should not be disregarded as "the blues".

You may notice stomach irritation, headaches, neck pain, muscle aches and if persistent these are signs of depression. Other signs are:

- Trouble paying attention/staying focused
- Drowsiness
- Feelings of worthlessness
- Trouble sleeping
- Changes in appetite
- Loss of energy
- Self pity
- Anxiety
- Sadness

Unfortunately, women often do not recognize symptoms in themselves, when family and friends do notice the change in your demeanor or that you are out of character. When family and friends start asking the question "are you alright?" then that's the time to discuss how you feel even though you may not recognize the signs.

The exact cause of depression is not known, however evidence points to many factors, including:

- ➢ Heredity
- ➢ Biochemical makeup
- ➢ Psychological makeup
- ➢ Stressful life events
- ➢ Fluctuating hormone levels
- ➢ Medical conditions and certain medications

Your reaction to life stressors can affect the normal level of chemical balance in the brain.

Things that can knock you off balance:

- ▪ Unemployment
- ▪ Finances
- ▪ Legal issues
- ▪ Ending relationships
- ▪ Illness or death in the family
- ▪ Sick children

- Out of control children
- Alcohol and Drugs

According to the National Institute of Mental Health, women with depressive illnesses do not all experience the same symptoms. How severe they are, how frequent, and how long they last will vary. It depends upon the individual.

Symptoms of Depression:

- ✓ Excessive Drinking
- ✓ Anti-Social Behavior
- ✓ Suicidal Thoughts
- ✓ Cutting Yourself
- ✓ Unexplained Lack of Motivation
- ✓ Anxiety

For a diagnosis of depression, the signs of depression should be present most of the day either daily or nearly daily for a least two weeks. In addition, the depressive symptoms need to cause clinically significant distress or impairment. Not the direct results from alcohol, drug, or medication. (depression guide.webMD.com)

There are several types of depression that can occur in women today, I have touched on very few symptoms to look at for awareness purposes only.

If you are a loved one recognize any of the combination of symptoms listed please seek medical attention. There are medications and exercises to help overcome and manage depression. You have to be suited with the right medication and this requires a doctor approval self medication is not good.

Depression treatment medication is constantly under development, most medications used for treatment are known as antidepressants, they help to prevent highs and lows in mood or emotional changes.
Today these medications are more suitable to the younger patient.

If you know someone who has depression, the first and most important thing you can do is to help her get an appropriate diagnosis and treatment. You may need to make an appointment on her behalf and go with her to see the doctor. Encourage her to stay in the treatment.

- Engage in conversation and listen
- Offer emotional support, patience, and understanding
- Never ignore comments about suicide, report to family or doctor
- Remind her that with time and treatment the depression will lift

If you feel that you are in a state of depression.

- Seek doctors care
- Engage in mild activity or exercise
- Break large task down to small ones
- Postpone important decisions
- Spend time with other people, share your emotions
- Be confident that the depression will lift with medication

Reference:
The National Institute of Mental Health (NIMH) a component of the U.S. Department of Health and Human Services

Historically, ***addiction*** has been defined as physical and/or psychological dependence on psychoactive substances (for example alcohol, tobacco, heroin, caffeine, and other drugs) which cross the blood-brain barrier once ingested, temporarily altering the chemical milieu of the brain. Broadly, addiction is defined as the continued use of a mood altering addictive substance or behaviors despite adverse consequences. (Wikipedia, the free encyclopedia)

Addiction can also be viewed as a continued involvement with a person that has negative consequences associated with them. This falls in line with abnormal psychological dependency on a partner that may cause chronic relapsing disorder (chaos) in your life.

 This happens when they bring their disorder into your household, for example, he has an addiction to drugs or alcohol which alters his attitude around your children, unemployed, uses your home to make illegal transactions, mood swings.

Addiction is a dependency applied to compulsions that are not always substance related.

Maintaining a healthy lifestyle is one of the best ways to keep you in good shape. There are several treatment programs throughout the city that can be successful in treating the addiction.

Without treatment, active drug addicts often end up dead, incarcerated, or in institutions. This behavior can be treated and you can live a normal and healthy life.

Without stability in your home not only do you suffer, your children suffer as well. Most children who grow up in a home with addictions tend to pick up their own addictions at an early age.

It is important to recognize your addition and seek the help you need for you and your family.

NOTES

_____

_____

_____

_____

_____

_____

_____

_____

_____

_____

Reflection

What new information did I learn today?

_____

_____

_____

_____

_____

_____

_____

_____

What am I doing right?

_____

_____

_____

_____

_____

_____

_____

_____

What needs to change and why?

_____

_____

_____

_____

_____

_____

_____

What are my next steps?

_____

_____

_____

_____

_____

_____

_____

_____

_____

Chapter 3

Domestic Violence/Healthy Relationships

In order to talk about domestic violence and begin to put an end to the violence that affects us as individuals, families and communities, we must first get a clear understanding of what domestic violence is and recognize that it may be called other terms, such as: family abuse, intimate partner violence, or dating abuse; but, is essential the same behavior which we must learn to recognize, and get a clear understanding of. It is not "marital conflict" "mutual abuse" a "lover's quarrel", or a private family matter.

Domestic violence is a pattern of violent or controlling behavior toward a current or former intimate or dating partner. Domestic violence is not just physical abuse. This is only one part of the whole system of abusive behaviors.

Domestic violence involves the use of several common behaviors. These are physical violence, intimidation, threats, isolation, emotional abuse, sexual abuse, the use of children, economic control, and/or male privilege.

Physical violence may include any number of unwanted physical behaviors against the intimate other, such as shoving or pushing, throwing objects, hitting or beating, strangulation, burning, using a weapon or restraining a partner from leaving.

Intimidation involves the use of gestures, looks, and actions that remind the victim of the batterer's potential and capacity for violence, such as smashing things, destroying the victim's property, abusing pets, and/or displaying weapons. Intimidation may also include abandoning or leaving a partner in a dangerous place or situation in order to demonstrate violent intent.

Emotional abuse involves the use of verbal insults which serve to undermine the victim's self-confidence, and discourage her from seeking to end the abusive relationship. With these tactics the abuser may strive to convince the victim that she is unattractive, a bad person, a bad parent or spouse, stupid, incapable, unemployable, promiscuous, and the cause of the abuse.

Sexual abuse which involves forced, unwanted sexual activity, sexual assault, sodomy, sexual mutilation, or forced or coerced prostitution, rape, not disclosing a sexually transmitted disease, making degrading sexual statements, accusing the victim of having affairs or of attempting to attract other sexual partners, forcing the victim to imitate pornography or pose for pornographic photography, and comparing the abused person's body to that of others.

Domestic Violence Affects Us All

On March 24, 1987 officers were dispatched to a domestic disturbance. Upon arrival at the scene dispatch advised that an ambulance had already left and taken the victim to Community Hospital East.

Upon officers going to Community Hospital a broadcast came over the police radio that the alleged suspect was possibly armed and dangerous, was driving a gold Cadillac and to proceed with caution because he may be headed to the hospital also.

When officers arrived at the hospital they were informed that a female had sustained an injury to her hand from a gunshot after an argument ensued over the female allowing a relative to care for their 3 month old child overnight.

In speaking with the victim, officers observed a fresh grazing wound to the victims' right hand. The victim stated she had worked an evening shift and had to be back at work the following morning and allowed her sister to take the child for an overnight stay.

When the child's father came home he became upset and angry that his "permission" was not asked for the child to leave the residence. A heated argument began and the male suspect grabbed a loaded revolver threatening to shoot the victim. When the male pointed the gun at the victim, she reached for the gun to keep the suspect from shooting her in the face. The suspect pulled the trigger and one shot penetrated the surface of Officer Bell's right hand.

That's my story…what's yours or someone you know and love…because no house is exempt.

I take domestic abuse personally and so should you. we have to stop "judging a book by its' cover" domestic violence affects people of all ages, race, gender, and economic class, that is why it can happen to you, just as it did to me.

Violence is destroying families and communities and we are not placing a high enough priority on the needs of those suffering from abuse. And, it is this neglect and silence of this "societal cancer" that is dangerous and sometimes can be lethal.

Not only as a detective with the police department and working cases have I experienced the lethality and death of victims of domestic abuse' but, also personally. My now 25 years old who was the 3 month old when my abuse began, had a dear friend and classmate killed in a double domestic homicide, here in the city of Indianapolis. A very close friend of mine was stalked by her intimate partner then shot in the face and killed in front of her 5 year old daughter. A co-worker who had a daughter born in 1986, the same year as my daughter, her daughter was brutally murdered and body mutilated.

- I believe that no human being deserves to be beaten or violated by another person.
- I believe that all person's have the right to live without fear, oppression, or sexual, emotional or physical abuse.
- I believe that batterers should be held accountable for their actions.
- I believe that the majority of victims of domestic violence are women and children;
  However everyone is affected by it and the solution involves us all taking an active stance against it; by educating ourselves-recognizing what it is and

knowing how to walk away from it. Not being silent about an abusive situation or thus, preventing the violence from ever happening. And, last but certainly not least is standing up for what we believe is right, no matter what the cost.

In preparing yourself to prevent becoming a victim, you must first empower yourself through education. After educating oneself, once you know better, you should do better by making wiser, well informed decisions and choices.

When I found myself in my abusive situation I constantly asked myself "how did I get in this place, what happened that I did not see this coming"? I questioned my ability to make good rational choice and decisions because I hadn't made a good choice in that bad relationship.

Well, all of this is a form of self doubt which we should never give in to. The more you doubt yourself the more you will unconsciously keep yourself in a negative mindset or mentality. Doing this allows the batterer to continue to have control over your life and empowers him and strips you of yourself worth and positive identity.

Pain comes into everyone's life, but misery is optional. The abusive relationship was painful, but I tried to keep a positive mindset and not give into the misery of what was happening in my life. I had a professional job, going to work every day solving everyone else's problems and taking domestic disturbance calls, and then going home to the same problems that I solved for others, but was unable to solve for myself.

My primary focus during this time was my daughter, who at the time was only 3 months old. I knew that she was all I had and that I had to strive to do all I could do for her because she was an infant and could not do for her. I had no support system because my family members and friends did not know of the violence that I was living in and I was too embarrassed to tell anyone. I feared that I would not be believed, I was trained to "protect" and serve and provided safety for the public and citizens, so why would I need help in protecting myself or my child.

I couldn't file a police report out of fear of losing my job or my personal business being gossiped about with other officers. I felt alone and certainly not educated or empowered.

Know that you are never alone and that empowerment comes from within. In order to escape the violence, I had to first recognize it. After that I changed my mindset and while still physically in the relationship, I changed my mentality about where I was at and began looking at my situation knowing that I would not live that way forever…in other words I saw a bigger picture and began mentally planning an "escape route to safety".

Please recognize that when you are in an abusive, violent relationship you are in an unsafe and unhealthy atmosphere not just for you, but for your children and other family members also.

The question is often asked, why women stay in abusive relationships. Well I believe the question should be why abusers abuse in relationships.

Statistics show that it takes a woman leaving 7 times before she stays gone out of an abusive relationship. I believe if we educate and empower we can reduce that number significantly.

Tools of Empowerment

- Education/Knowledge
- Skills
- Strength
- Courage
- Support
- Goals
- Morals
- Family/Friends
- Church
- Good habits
- Time management

- ➢ Control your own destiny
- ➢ Life purpose
- ➢ Passion
- ➢ Stand up to obstacles
- ➢ Employment
- ➢ Knowing your resources

Written By:
Detective Marta Bell
Indianapolis Metropolitan Police Department

Notes

_____
_____
_____
_____
_____
_____
_____
_____
_____
_____
_____
_____
_____

Reflection

What new information did I learn today?

_____
_____
_____
_____
_____
_____
_____
_____

What am I doing right?

_____
_____
_____
_____
_____
_____
_____
_____

What needs to change and why?

_____

_____

_____

_____

_____

_____

_____

_____

What are my next steps?

_____

_____

_____

_____

_____

_____

_____

_____

_____

_____

_____

_____

_____

Chapter 4

Empowerment and the Benefits

Self-Empowerment can give you the ambition you need to get that promotion you've been seeking, the will to create new goals for yourself and the drive to achieve them.

Self-Empowerment removes the weakness of human spirit set in your mind, the feeling that you are nobody special, the thought that no one cares about you, even thinking that you can't do any better are all feelings and thoughts that keep you from rising to the top.

Bad attitudes and even worse love cycles can be attributed to character flaws and emotional disorders.

I do understand that you sometimes lack the willpower and energy to make the necessary changes to get your life on track, but in order to have that fulfilled and satisfying life you have to do something other than what you've always done.

It's time to internalize those emotions and make them work for you in a positive way. Simply reading a book or going to a seminar is not going to get it; you must be motivated to make the transformation.

Learn to utilize the resources that are available, take advantage of the opportunities afforded to you. You have to subconsciously wrap your mind around the fact that there is a better you on the inside fighting to get out.

Women tend to not what to help each other or turn up their noses at someone who is not in the same position, when we are all just one pay check away from being in the very same position or if someone had not looked upon them with favor.

Women you have a boldness about you that can greatly enhance your ability to bring about enormous improvements in your life. You must generate lots of energy and invest it into yourself.

Make a statement take a stance that you will turn your life around, and commit it to your heart.

Set short-term goals that are obtainable, after you obtain that very first goal treat yourself (i.e.

go to a movie, read a book, take a break) and don't let anyone steal your joy.

When we obtain the things in life that we set out to do, it is such an empowering feeling of accomplishment and you deserve to be proud of yourself. After you attain those short-term goals then move on to a bigger goal, we all have restored energy that we have not tapped into.

In order to be self-empowered it has to be an accomplishment that make a difference to you, that ultimately makes a difference to someone else for example: I have never written a book before, however it was in my heart to help empower other women who are in the same place that I came from but I could not find a book to deliver what I wanted, so my dear friend said "why don't you write the book"?

Once I thought about it and thought if I can reach just one woman and empower, encourage, and mentor her into making a better life for her then it would be worth it. I had to dig deep to find that untapped energy in me to write and promote this book.

This book is an accomplishment that made a difference to me that I hope will ultimately make a difference to you

Unlock the potential within your inner self, how can you tap and use the source of energy in you to make a difference in your life, which will empower you to be the best that you can be.

You have to start with positive thoughts; start by programming your mind to use a bigger portion of your brain to create thoughts that can generate energy and create changes in your pattern of thinking.

Your thoughts measure your success.

- What inspires you?
- What keeps you wanting a healthy lifestyle while others drink and smoke?
- What is that one thing that you truly want to accomplish?
- Are you a role model to your children?
- Where do you want to be in five (5) years?
- What type of wife do you want to be?

All those people who you feel have made it in life had no bigger brain then you or I, the difference is how they made use of their minds. Our thoughts are very important and shape our lives.

If you change your thinking pattern and access the outcome you wish to obtain, then you can change your lifestyle forever. Your actions and future are caused by your thoughts; and comes from both the conscious and subconscious mind.

Once you've made up in your mind what you truly want in life, the sky is the limit to what you can set your mind to.

Put pen to paper start writing out a plan for your life, and start by removing any negative influences in your life, these influences and people will destroy any chance you have of succeeding.

To begin know the difference between negative and positive thoughts. For example, saying: "this is impossible" or "it can't be done", zaps all the energy you just put into this project. This will cause you to stop trying and prevent you from reaching your goal.

Positive thoughts bring about higher productivity, higher energy levels, and achievement. Encourage yourself to reach your goal, set goals within your limitations to start, and keep lifting yourself up until you reach that long term goal that you've set your heart on. Tell yourself anything is possible when I set my mind to it. (Dr. Greg Frost, Director of Charged Audio)

NOTES

_____

_____

_____

_____

_____

_____

_____

_____

_____

_____

_____

Reflection

What new information did I learn today?

_____

_____

_____

_____

_____

_____

_____

_____

What am I doing right?

_____

_____

_____

_____

_____

_____

_____

_____

_____

_____

What needs to change and why?

_____

_____

_____

_____

_____

_____

_____

_____

What are my next steps?

_____

_____

_____

_____

_____

_____

_____

_____

_____

_____

Chapter 5

Breaking Bad Habits

A habit is any action that we have performed so often that it becomes almost an involuntary response. If you consider this habit to be undesirable then you may label it a "bad habit".

They say old habits are hard to break, I would have to agree with this statement, however, once my back was up against the wall a few times I knew I had to break those bad habits.

It's all about choices. The only way to stick with bad habits in today's time is though denial.

Our choices in life tell the story of who we are; you have to decide how the choice makes you feel? If it makes you feel bad then it's a bad choice and if you continue with the choice it becomes a bad habit, and it now makes you feel bad about yourself.

Bad habits fill a need and in order to break those bad habits you have to make a choice either one that will make you feel good or one that will make you feel bad it's up to you...it's all about the choices we make.

Bad habits also affect our lifestyle and prohibit us from living a healthy life. Some behaviors are learned which include some bad habits, but it is important to know that learned behavior can be unlearned.

Bad habits affect your children, your environment, your living conditions and so much more. You must learn to substitute the bad habits for good habits.

Most common bad habits:

- Smoking
- Emotional eating
- Gossip
- Nail biting
- Procrastinating

Smoking

Even though there are so many health risk and complications with smoking it is still the most common bad habit most people suffer with, and one of the most difficult habits to break. I would suggest getting outside help to assist with smoking, including a support group.

Emotional Eating

Most women who struggle with their weight have an emotional eating disorder; this is also a side effect of depression. This emotion has to be tackled head on and even though overeating is a bad habit, this could be directly connected to depression. It can be controlled though diet and exercise but I would also suggest you find something exciting or energetic to replace those cravings. I do understand that it takes will power to overcome this disorder, it helps to start a journal to track everything that you put in your mouth daily and the emotion you have when you crave. You would be surprised at what and how much you're consuming once you see it in writing and writing your emotions help identify why you feel the need to eat.

Gossip

If you talk more about other people's problem than you do your own, then you could be considered a gossip. To some women gossip is just a way to interact with conversation, but the conversations can become destructive to others and you need to stop.

Discussing others peoples business to someone other than that person should make you feel uncomfortable, and think about what if someone was discussing your business without your knowledge how it would make you feel.

Gossip can be very hurtful and most often times taken out of context of what the reality of the situation is. Remember if it's not for the good of another person to lift them up, or give assistance then it probably couldn't be discussed.

Nail Biting

Nail biting can be a very ugly habit, but it can also be very dangerous, this is a good way to contract infections in your mouth from bacteria or viruses that are under your fingernails.

Nail biting is common in a lot of women and children to relieve stress, boredom, hunger, nervousness, and a host of other reasons the point is it is a very nasty habit.

Nail biting was a habit I had as a young girl and because I continued to bite my nails I always felt like my hands were so ugly. My mother would put hot sauce on my fingers to discourage me from biting, but nothing worked. In my junior year in high school my mother encouraged me to paint my nails and brought polishes, nail files, the whole kit for me to start taking care of my nails and once they started growing I noticed how nice my hands looked. That was over 30 years ago I still take care of my nails and it is definitely a stress reliever; taking time to polish and file my nails takes my mind off other things.

Procrastinating

This is one that I have certainly been guilty of, to avoid the things I really did not want to deal with, therefore, it's always in the forefront of my mind to address issues and situations that intimidate me immediately.

Procrastination is an avoidance behavior and can sometimes be caused by not wanting to deal with the consequences, this is one that many women are guilty of and it could be something as simple as not taking care of the noise you hear coming from the engine, because you feel that it could lead to something worse, therefore, you avoid it all together. Bad habits are emotionally and physically not healthy especially for women because of your hormonal make up, but with some will power those bad habits can be reversed.

How to Cope With Stress:

This can be a powerful tool in your fight against depression.

- o Manage anxiety through deep breathing
- o Relaxation Exercises for a minimum of 20 minutes 3 times per week reduces stress
- o Avoid caffeine, it is a stimulant
- o Avoid alcohol and drugs, this can quickly become an addiction and creates double the trouble
- o Look for the positive in every situation
- o Unresolved emotions can lead to nightmares or physical illness, share your feelings with someone you trust or
- o Write down your emotions it's a safe and private way to release them

- If you find that a relationship causes you stress....end it
- Really listen to what others are saying, verses getting upset because you do not agree, find areas of common ground
- Seek social support
- Smile more often...it makes you feel better

NOTES

_____

_____

_____

_____

_____

_____

_____

_____

_____

_____

_____

_____

_____

Chapter 6

How to Build Trust and Bridge the Communication Gap with Law Enforcement

The Indianapolis Metropolitan Police Department would like to increase our communication skills within our service district to help bring about positive changes in our relationship with all citizens in our service area. Our goal is to tear down those negative barriers and build respect and trust between law enforcement officers and the communities in which we serve.

In an effort to achieve our goal we want to empower women to assume responsibility in your neighborhood to improve the quality of life, as well as increase law enforcement officers' knowledge of understanding socialization issues and empowerment development.

Values:

- ❖ To enhance law enforcement officers' community policing skills
- ❖ To productively engage with the community
- ❖ To empower women to stand on their own and not be taken for granted or taken advantage of
- ❖ To effect communication strategies involving de-escalation, crisis intervention, and problem-solving skills.

Vision:

- To lay a solid foundation that empowers law enforcement and women with a voice to come together and brainstorm solutions, with a proactive attitude toward safer neighborhoods.
- To facilitate ways for women to learn about career paths, how to train for the job you want, how to write a resume, how to dress for success.
- To promote relationships that foster reciprocal obligation to promote safety in the homes with children

- To link the women involved with resources available to assist with their quality of life issues.

Now you have heard from IMPD and what our goals are, now we would like to know what you want to see happen and what role you will play in the process?

There is a purpose for you to become involved in tearing down strongholds, and building relationships with your local law enforcement agency. I am certain that you have police officers that you see on a regular basis in your area where you live and you don't know their names and they don't know you?

Becoming involved with the police in your area is a self-help cooperative effort to reduce crime and the fear of crime in your neighborhood and is achieved by citizens such as yourself and law enforcement working together.
Believe it or not we really do care about the safety of our citizens and we want to

help you stay safe and a safe place for your children to play.

Now you can be either part of the problem or part of the solution? You can help by getting to know the police in your area stop and say hello or wave as they ride down the street. This lets our officers know that you are approachable because we don't get a lot of friendly hellos while on patrol.

Remember we are not the enemy and also police are people too, they sometimes come to work on a bad day, or had been up all night with a sick kid, there are many reasons why they may seem a little distant, but don't let this stop you from speaking or saying hello.
Get to know the officers that patrol your area, and once you bridge that communication gap you will feel more comfortable discussing neighborhood concerns or identifying problems in your neighborhood.

Our goal is to make you safe in your home, but we cannot do that if you are a part of the problem, so my question to you is are you a part of the solution?

We welcome new and innovative ideas for safer neighborhoods, and because you live in the neighborhood and we are just passing through it is important for you to have input in your community on what we can do to make your neighborhood safer.

Cleaning up a neighborhood starts with you, you are our eyes and ears. The concerned citizen is the criminal's worst enemy because neighborhood unity can deter crime.

- Report to police illegal or suspicious activities
- Testify in court if you are a witness to a crime
- Join neighbors to help correct situations that threaten peace and safety in your community
- Don't become a victim, be a "good" neighbor, act against crime

RESOURCE DIRECTORY

IN AN Emergency _____ Call 911

Any crime happening right ***NOW***
Suspicious Activity ***IN PROGRESS***
Fire/Medical Emergencies/Fight/Person Shot/
Stabbed

Non-Emergency _____ 327 -3811

Courtesy number for incidents *NOT*
OCCURRING RIGHT NOW

There may be a delayed response since 911
Emergencies take priority

Connect 2 Help _____ Dial 2-1-1
www.Connect2Help.org
317-926-4357
For information about...
Food. Counseling . Health Care . Clothing .
Employment . Shelter
Support Groups . Volunteering . Parenting .
Housing . Legal Aid
Recreation . Education . And More

24 hours a day ... A United Way Partner Agency

Indianapolis Metropolitan Police Department

IMPD Headquarters (50 N. Alabama St.) ....
327-3282
North District (3120 E. 30th St.) ....
327-6100
East District (201 N. Shadeland Av.) ....
327-6200
Southeast District (1150 S. Shelby St.) ....
327-6300
Southwest District (551 N. King Av.) ....
327-6400
Downtown District (39 W, Jackson Pl ste 500)..
327-6500
Northwest District (3820 N. Industrial Blvd) ....
327-6600
DOPE Hotline ....
327-3673
GANG Hotline ....
898-4264
Traffic Enforcement ....
327-6525
Animal Control ....
327-1391

Crime Stoppers
.... 262-TIPS
Metro Drug Task Force
.... 631-1826
Safe Streets Task Force
.... 327-2030
Citizen's Complaint Office
.... 327-3440
Street Blocking Permit
.... 327-4849
Victim Assistance (IMPD) ....
327-3331

Mayor's Action Center ....
327-4622
To report abandoned vehicles, weeds, graffiti,
street maintenance, traffic signal repair, street
sweeping, illegal dumping, dead animal
removal and other city service requests

Mayor's Neighborhood Liaison ....
327-5014

Marion Co. Health Department ....
221-2000
Housing & Neighborhood Health ....
221-2150

Marion Co. Prosecutor's Office ....
327-3522
Court Watch (MCPO) ....
327-5210

City/County Council Office ....
327-4242

Child Abuse Hotline ....
1-800-800-5556
Adult Protective Services ....
327-1403
Rape Crisis/Suicide Hotline ....
251-7575
Poison Control Center ....
962-2323
IPL Security Light Information ....
261-8653
Keep Indianapolis Beautiful ....
264-7555
Indy Parks Department ....
327-0000
Indianapolis Neighborhood ....
920-0330
    Resource Center

Helpline ....
926-4357
For information about food, counseling, health
care, clothing, employment, shelter, support
groups, recreation, child care, legal aid,
parenting, education and more

Marion County Sheriff ....
327-1700

NOTES

_____

_____

_____

_____

_____

_____

_____

_____

_____

_____

_____

Reflection

What new information did I learn today?

_____

_____

_____

_____

_____

_____

_____

_____

What am I doing right?

_____

_____

_____

_____

_____

_____

_____

_____

What needs to change and why?

_____
_____
_____
_____
_____
_____
_____

What are my next steps?

_____
_____
_____
_____
_____
_____
_____
_____
_____
_____
_____
_____

Chapter 7

A New Direction

I once read an article regarding changing a person's life and it outlined four (4) steps we had to take to make a lasting change in our life.

It talked about changing your belief, which would lead to a change of behavior, followed by a change of results which leads to a <u>New Direction.</u>

1. Belief ... about the situation! You have to believe the situation is real....this leads to...
2. Behavior ... how does it affect you? ... leads to...
3. Results ... you have to change what you've been doing to get the results you want... leads to...
4. <u>New Direction</u> ... this awareness of your present situation will <u>lead</u> you in a new direction if you empower yourself and

take control of the things you allow in your life.

In order to move forward you must first choose to live with purpose and passion, envision the new you with self-worth, self-love, self-respect, and self-esteem. Change your belief about yourself.

Just think of how powerful you would be, achieving personal growth begins with being secure in who you are, always remember that you can only control yourself and not the actions of others, so put your concentration on being positive. Change your behavior.

Start with:

> Positive people in your circle of friends
> Stop cussing and fussing
> Arguing changes nothing
> Screaming and yelling

All these things zap your energy and cause unnecessary stress.

Because you have the power over yourself, this gives you the ability to empower yourself, to be the best person you want to be in life.

Empowerment comes from effectively learning how to make good decisions and make healthy choices. Expect better results.

Start by writing a list of things you would like to accomplish, set time lines and check off each item as it is completed. Writing helps to motivate you to accomplish what you put on paper. These should be the desires of your heart and this list should inspire you to meet the challenge you placed on yourself.

Be encouraged and know that you can do anything you set your mind to.

Remember believe, change your behavior, look for positive results, and start moving in a new direction.

A Women's Worth...

Is there such...

Or do we not give ourselves the valve that we so rightfully deserve...

From our inner spirit...To our vivacious curves...

Worth that does hold value...

Values that not even the naked eye can see...

The value that starts from the heart...

Beats from the soul...

And continues with our flow...

Know your worth when no one else does...

Know your worth just because...

You are special...Beautiful in every way...

This will remain with each given day...

To love thyself and to continue falling in love with you.

Written by: Ms. Dawn Rivers

NOTES

_____

_____

_____

_____

_____

_____

_____

_____

_____

_____

_____

<u>GOALS</u>

1. _____

   _____

2. _____

   _____

3. _____

   _____

4. _____

   _____

5. _____
   _____

<u>CHALLENGES</u>

1. _____
   _____
   _____

2. _____
   _____
   _____

3. _____
   _____
   _____

4. _____
   _____
   _____

5. _____
   _____
   _____

Reflection

What new information did I learn today?

_____

_____

_____

_____

_____

_____

_____

What am I doing right?

_____

_____

_____

_____

_____

_____

_____

_____

_____

What needs to change and why?

_____

_____

_____

_____

_____

_____

_____

_____

What are my next steps?

_____

_____

_____

_____

_____

_____

_____

_____

_____

_____

_____

_____

Chapter 8

Dressing for Success/How to Write a Resume

Dressing for success is the way to the utmost respect and consideration when interviewing for a job.

1. Be conservative, you do not want to go into a business with attitude written all over your clothing (i.e. hot pink, red, blue jeans, etc.) choose colors that are neutral, grey, black, and dark blue are always good choices. Wear a suit with coordinating blouse.
2. Well- groomed hair (no wild colors, a 27 piece in 27 colors, lint balls, etc.) remove hair from your face and if it's stacked tone it down a little.
3. Be very careful with visible body piercings, tattoos, tight clothing, these

things can send the wrong message. I know we shouldn't judge but an employer may view you as trouble not even knowing your work ethics.

4. If you are one that like a lot of make-up...tone it down, clean under your nails (you'd be surprised how many people look for dirt under your nails)
5. No gum, candy, in your mouth, fresh breath, and brushed teeth
6. Wear minimal jewelry
7. Arrive at least 30 minutes early, to readjust, and promptness is very important to any employer

How you dress sets the tone of the interview, first impressions are very important and can cost you the position you want, remember you are being judged once you walk into the interview room

Take deep breaths and calm yourself before you walk into the interview room

Do not let the impressions on the interviewers face intimidate you, often times when people are listening to you and trying to comprehend what you are saying they tend to not look so pleasant.

Stay focused, be professional at all times, and don't try to look or sound like anyone else, just be the best YOU.

Resume Writing Tips:

Resumes should be short and to the point...

Resumes are now being viewed electronically by many businesses now so they are not looking for novels explaining every position you've ever held.

Skills and achievements should be listed in bullet point form early on in the resume to set you aside from everyone else, keeping the document short and to the point

Resumes should be two pages are less with focus on most recent employment, with emphasis on promotions and achievement

The Department of Labor suggests if you have been unemployed for a lengthy period of time, list volunteer experiences to demonstrate experience.

Managers will scan your resume for just about 10 minutes to see if you are right for the job.

www.resume-now.com can build your resume in minutes

- It's fast and easy, guides you through step-by-step
- Resume templates for all jobs and industries
- One-click resume formatting for the professional look you want
- Writing help includes pre-written sample phrases
- Now with cover letters

I actually went on this website to see just how easy it was and it can help you build a very professional resume in just minutes, with the unique text tuner it allows you to choose from hundreds of expert-written examples.

It is a step-by-step process that can create, design and customize your resume to make it stand out.

Cost to use website:

$4.95 allows you 7 day access

$7.95 per month

The website is just a tool, you can also go to the public library in your area to get assistance and examples on writing a resume, the important thing is to emphasize your most impressive selling points and paint a positive picture of your accomplishments without listing job duties.

When you get into job duties this takes up a lot of space to outline what your job entailed.

Many employers are using the internet to build online communities and social media networking sites to find qualified candidates, you have to be very careful what you post on face book because employers are now relying on social media networking to allow them to see the true person they may be considering as a new hire.

If there are things on your social media networks that could possibly keep you from getting a job, then you should clean it up before you start to seek employment.

NOTES

_____

_____

_____

_____

_____

_____

_____

_____

_____

_____

_____

_____

_____

_____

_____

Chapter 9

Resources

This chapter was included to provide you with resources that are available for women.

1. Goodwill Industry 1635 W. Michigan Street (317) 524-4313
   Services include:
   - Senior Community Service Employment Program (SCSEP) a program offered to low income senior citizens 55 years and older looking to get back into the workforce
   - Paid training
   - Disability services, helps with job search, resume building, job search

online, workshops to refine job
search skills.

- Employment Center that helps the
community with job search
assistance, resume building, online
job search, active job leads,
workshops to refine skill levels,
computer classes, resource center
with computers Monday thru Friday
8am to 5pm **(317) 524 - 4325**
- Guides to help you through steps to
complete goals in employment,
education, housing and
transportation
- For more information about
workshops **(317) 524-4260**

2. Connect 2 Help Dial 2-1-1...Food,
Counseling, HealthCare, Clothing,
Employment, Shelter, Support Groups,
Volunteering, Parenting, Housing, Legal
Aid, Recreation, Education, and more.
3. Commercial Services is another program
thru Goodwill for individuals with many
barriers to employment by providing
warehouse, janitorial and groundskipping
paid on the job training and life skill

classes as well as ex-offender with felonies paid training for more information: contact Trelles Evans **(317) 524-3957**

4. Metropolitan High School (IMET), started a charter school for troubled kids from 9th to 12th grade for more information: contact Scott Bess **(317) 524-4501**

5. The Excel Center, an adult High School, for individuals who are interested in getting a high school diploma or accredited GED, it is free of charge for more information: contact Nicollete Jones **(317) 524-4287**

6. Nurse Family Partnership, to serve first time moms who are under poverty level with the pregnancy to make sure she has a safe and natural child birth, nurse visits in the home until the baby is two (2) years old for more information: contact Lissa Crane **(317) 524-4407**

7. Work One Indy 2525 N. Shadeland Avenue, employment, training, resumes, workshops and more.
www.workoneindy.gov

8. Affordable Housing - contact Regina Baxter 317-258-3060

9. Emergency Housing/Domestic Violence Shelter contact Regina Baxter @ 317-258-

3060 women & children only. No felonies allowed.

10. G.E.D. and other trainings contact Kim Bostic @ Mt. Carmel Church 317-890-2740 ext. 23

11. G.E.D. and Tabe Test for funding through Work One East Office contact Walker Career Center 317-532-6150

12. Parenting and Fathers class/Domestic Violence contact: Fathers and Families Center located at 3800 N. Franklin Road

13. Food pantry, Reentry, Women in Motion, Head Start Program, Community Groups, Medical Clinic, Computer and Resume Writing, Goodwill Industries, CAFÉ 8902 East 38th Street

14. Alpha Resources provides treatment and classes 16th and Ritter Ave contact: Mrs. Denise 317-353-8494

15. Transitional Housing for Women only @ Wailing Women Win contact: Minister Aritha Luster 317-926-5357

16. Utility Assistance if Domestic Violence related contact: Regina Baxter 317-258-3060 for any other assistance contact Lawrence or Warren Trustee

17. Pathway Resources located in Amber Woods Apartments 10119 John Marshall Drive: Free computer lab and internet access, Youth Development, Employment Separation and Job Readiness, and Summer Program 317-890-9816
18. New Beginning's Ministries inside Washington Square Mall contact: Pastor Christopher Thorpe offers childcare, ministry, youth and family groups
19. Fervent Prayer Ministries 10512 East 38th Street child care services contact: Mrs. Peaches 317-899-3750
20. Mt. Carmel Church 9610 East 42nd Street child care services contact: Kim Bostic 317-890-2740
21. Indiana Access to Recovery 402 W. Washington Street, Room W353 Division of Mental Health and Addiction dmha.atr3application@fssa.in.gov
22. Family and Social Services Administration 402 W. Washington Street , P.O. Box 7083 www.IN.gov/fssa
23. Dress for Success 850 N. Meridian Street (317) 940-3737

Citations :

Indianapolis Metropolitan Police Department
Chief Paul Ciesielski
Deputy Chief Scott Haslar
Commander James Water
Detective Marta Bell
IMPD Crime Watch ... Resources
Ms. LaTonya Littlejohn...Heart's Landing
Apartments
Mr. Michael Batic ... Carriage House
Apartments
La Keisha Jackson ... Amber Woods
Apartments
Eastlawn Wesleyan Church...Pastor Thomas
Johnson Greater Works and Urban Ministries
Pastor
CAFÉ' (Community Alliance of the Far Eastside,
Inc.)
Far Eastside Weed & Seed ... publication of
books
Mrs. Regina Baxter .... Far eastside Resources
Yaily M. Padron ... Goodwill Industries of
Central Indiana
Ms. Dawn Rivers ... poem

References:

Kandra Cherry – about.com/psychology
John D. Mayer – Psychologist at the University of New Hampshire
Peter Salovey – President of the Society for General Psychology and treasurer of the International Society for research on emotion.
University of Iowa Health Care
Depression guide.webMD.com
Wikipedia, the free encyclopedia
The National Institute of Mental Health (NIMH) a component of the U.S. Department of Health and Human Services
Dr. Greg Frost, Director of Charged Audio
Resume – now.com
Department of Labor

www.ingramcontent.com/pod-product-compliance
Lightning Source LLC
Chambersburg PA
CBHW021837020426
42334CB00014B/670